THE BABY BOOMER'S

EYE
CHART

A VISUAL ACUITY PROGRAM
FOR THE MIDDLE-AGED

BY **DRS. KAT A. RAQUE** AND **KENT SEAWELL**

RUNNING PRESS
PHILADELPHIA · LONDON

© 2007 by becker&mayer!

First published in the United States in 2007 by

Running Press Book Publishers

All rights reserved under the Pan-American

and International Copyright Conventions

Printed in China

9   8   7   6   5   4   3   2   1

Digit on the right indicates the number of this printing

Library of Congress Control Number: 2007923342

ISBN-13: 978-0-7624-3198-4

ISBN-10: 0-7624-3198-9

Cover image: Retrofile/Getty Images

Design: Todd Bates and Paul Barrett

Editorial: Meghan Cleary

Production Coordination: Shirley Woo

The Baby Boomer's Eye Chart is produced by

becker&mayer!, Bellevue, Washington.

www.beckermayer.com

This book may be ordered by mail from the publisher.

Please include $2.50 for postage and handling.

But try your bookstore first!

Running Press Book Publishers

2300 Chestnut Street

Philadelphia, PA 19103-4371

Visit us on the web!

www.runningpress.com

After years of treating patients who claim to be "young" despite their bat-like vision, it has become clear to us that most simply refuse to face this medical certitude: While failing eyesight may be the most obvious symptom of middle age, it is by no means the only one. In a wholehearted effort to bring true clarity to the Baby Boomer generation, we've created this collection of self-administrable eye exams—multi-purpose charts which test not only your visual acuity, but also your grip on reality, your patience, and even your sense of humor. (If you don't have a couple of laughs while reading these, you are most definitely an old curmudgeon!)

━━━━━━━━ **W A R N I N G :** ━━━━━━━━

Taking an eye chart exam geared for the middle-aged often results in frantic and foolhardy behavior, including desperate attempts to squeeze into that slinky dress you've held on to since college, or ad hoc workouts in the garage followed by peacock-like displays of virility while mowing the lawn. Please, resist the urge to partake in such activity, as it will confuse and frighten your friends and neighbors and, trust us on this one, really piss off your kids.

— Drs. Kat A. Raque & Kent Seawell

DISCLAIMER: *The Baby Boomer's Eye Chart* is not intended for diagnostic use. If you are worried that you might be middle-aged, simply look in the mirror.

I

FON

LYIHAD

MYGLASS

ESICOULD

READWHAT

THISSAYSBUT

FORNOWIWILL

JUSTSMILEANDNOD

N

O W T

H A T I H A

V E B E N T A L L

T H E W A Y O V E R I

———

W O N D E R I F T H E R

E ' S A N Y T H I N G E L S E

———

I S H O U L D P I C K U P

W H I L E I ' M D O W N H E R E

H
ONE
YIDO
NOTCA

REWHERE

YOUGOJU

STSOLONG

ASYOUDON'T

MAKEMECOMEALONG

E
VER
YDAYI
WAKEUP

LOOKINGMO
REANDMORE

LIKEMYDRIVE
R'SLICENSEPICTURE

N
OW
THAT
I'VERET
IREDIPLAN

TOBECOME

ANINVENTOR

MYFIRSTIDEAIS

AMUTEBUTTONFORMYWIFE

M
Y 4 0
1 K N E E D
S O N L Y 3 5

M O R E Y E A R S

━━━━━━━━━━━━━━━━━━━━━

O F F U N D I N G

O H M Y G O D I ' L L

━━━━━━━━━━━━━━━━━━━━━

N E V E R B E A B L E

T O E A T O U T A G A I N

M

YSEX

UALFAN

TASYISBE

INGPHYSICA

LLYABLETOHAVE

SEXEVERAGAIN

OREVENWANTINGTO

DOES IT COUNT AS DIETING IF INSTEAD OF APPETIZERS YOU EAT METAMUCIL?

THE WORST IS WHEN YOUR CLOTHES GO OUT OF STYLE ALL OVER AGAIN

I
STI
LLLIKE
MYMUSIC
LOUD, MAN
OTHERWISE
I CAN'T HEAR IT

I

TAK

EMORE

DRUGSNOW

THANIDID

BACKINHIGH

SCHOOLANDCO

LLEGECOMBINED

O
N T
H E B R
I G H T S I D E
M Y H E A T I N G
B I L L S H A V E G O N E
D O W N S I N C E I S T A R T E D
H A V I N G T H E S E H O T F L A S H E S

T

HIN

GSWERE

LOOKING

ROSYTHIS

MORNINGUNTI

LIREALIZED

I HAD WASHED MY

GLASSES IN PEPTO BISMOL

I
QUIT
WORRY
INGABOUT
MYCHILDREN

SOMUCHONCE

I LOST TRACK

OF WHO WAS WHO

A

TT H

ISAGE

I'M NOT

AFRAID

OFANYTHING

EXCEPTTHEIRS.

I
MIG
HTCO
NSIDER
USINGVIA
GRAIFITCAME
WITHABETTER
LOOKINGWIFE

I
RE
FUSE
TOMOVE

INTOARETIRE
MENTHOMETHAT

ALLOWSVISITS

FROMFAMILYMEMBERS

I
CAN
NOTSA
YIMISS

BEINGYO

UNGBECAUSE

HONESTLYIDON'T

REMEMBERMUCHOFIT

I

USE

DTOG

ETOUTOF

SPEEDING

TICKETSBYSH

OWINGSOMESKIN

NOWIJUSTTHREATENTO

N

OON

ETAK

ESRESP

ONSIBIL

ITYFORANY

THINGANYMORE

I BLAME THE YOUTH

I

M A

Y N O T

GOOUTMU

CHANYMORE

BUTMYBAC

KSUREDOES

I

T U S

E D T O

B E I C O U

L D S T A N D M Y

W I F E W I T H O

U T B E I N G D R U N K

WHATAMISAY

ING, NO I COULDN'T

I
COU
LDHAVE
RETIRED
ATFIFTYIF

MYKIDSHAD

NOTBEENSO

INSISTENTUPON

GOINGTOCOLLEGE

I
ON
LYS
MOKE

AFTER SEX
SINCE THAT'S

THE ONLY WAY
I KNOW TO QUIT

GETTING

ET

TING

RID OF

FACIAL WRI

NKLESISEASY

ALLIHAVETODO

ISTAKEOFFMYBRA

I

U S

E D T O

S C O L D

M Y K I D S F

O R F A R T I N G

N O W T H E Y

S C O L D M E

THE SEDAYS AGOOD TRIP IS ONE THAT DOESN'T INVOLVE VISITING THE IN LAWS

M

Y W

I F E M

A Y B E Y

O U N G A T

————————————

H E A R T B U T

I T ' S H E R F A C E

————————————

T H A T I H A V E T O

L O O K A T E V E R Y D A Y

C

OOK

INGUS

EDTOBEA

TOTALDRAG

SODIDVACUUM

INGANDLAUNDRY

SOMETHINGS

NEVERCHANGE

I
USE
DTOSPE
NDSPRING
BREAKINFLO

RIDATOESC
APEMYPARENTS

NOWI'MRETIRING

THERETOESCAPEMYKIDS

I

N O

LONG

ERCARE

ABOUTTHE

WAYILOOK

WHENIGOOUT

MYHUSBANDSAYS

THAT'SADAMNGOODTHING

M

Y D

O C T O

R S A Y S

I H A V E C

A N C E R A N D

E A R L Y O N S E T

A L Z H E I M E R ' S B U T A T

L E A S T I D O N ' T H A V E C A N C E R

I

NEV

ERTHO

UGHTI'DS

EEMYDAUGH

———

TERASHAPPYAS

SHEWASATHERWED

———

DINGUNTILSHECHUCK

EDMEINARETIREMENTHOME

I

DO

NOT

NEED G

LASSES

I JUST NEED

LONGER ARMS

I
LO
VEM
YWIFE
BUTWHEN

IOCCASI

ONALLYFOR

GETABOUTHERI

LOVETHATEVENMORE

I
CA
NSTIL
LDRINKA

NYONEUNDER

THETABLEASLONG

ASTHERE'SAPIL

LOWORTWODOWNTHERE

E

VER

YTHIN

GIEVER

NEEDEDTO

KNOWILEARNED

INKINDERGARTEN

ANDFORGOTLASTYEAR

I

THA

SBEENA

LONGTIM

ESINCEIGOT

LUCKYBUTTO

DAYITONLY

TOOKMEFIFTEEN

MINUTESTOFINDTHECAR

WHEN I RETIRE

I'M TAKING MY WIFE

TO PARIS AND

LEAVING HER THERE

T
HE
ONLY
ONEWHO
GETSTURN
EDONINOUR
BEDROOMANY

MOREISJAYLENO

T
HE
WIFE
DOESN'T
MINDTHAT

IGOTOSTRIP

CLUBSANYMORE

SHEKNOWSICAN'T

SEEANYTHINGANYWAY

I
FIN
ALLY
MADEM
OTHERPR

OUDNOWTH

ATMYDATEBOOK

ISFULLOFDOCTORS

WANTINGTOEXAMINEMYBREASTS

I
AL
WAYS
THOUGHT

MOWING THE

LAWN WAS SUCH

A PAIN IN THE ASS UN

TIL I HAD A COLONOSCOPY

I
T U
S E D
T O B E T H
E P O L I C E

W H O T O L D M E
T O S L O W D O W N

B U T N O W I T ' S
M Y D O C T O R

I

FOR

GOTIT

WASOUR

ANNIVERSA

RYLASTWEEK

BUTNOPROBLEM

BECAUSESODIDSHE

THE

YSAY

AGECO

MESWITH

WISDOMBUTI

WOULDPREFERA

FUNCTIONINGBLADDER

I
N B
E D I
F E E L

L I K E A T W

E N T Y Y E A R

O L D B U T I S E T

T L E F O R M Y W I F E

I
HAV
EPLEN
TYOFNAM

ESINMYADD

RESSBOOKBUT

MOSTOFTHEM

ENDWITHM.D.

I
U S
E D T O
W O R R Y
A B O U T N O T

G E T T I N G E N O U

G H A C T I O N A F T E R

---

4 0 B U T B A C K T H E N I D I D

N ' T K N O W I H A D A P R O S T A T E

I
RE
ALLY
CAN'TAF
FORDTOH
AVEANOTHER
HEARTATTACK
MYHMOSAIDSO

I
USE
DTOGET
DISCOUN
TSBECAUSE

OFMYFETCH

INGGOODLOOKS

BUTMYA.A.R.P.CARDIS

MUCHMORERELIABLENOW

I WOULD LOVE TO CALL MY KIDS TO THANK THEM FOR BUYING ME THIS CELL PHONE BUT I DON'T EVEN KNOW HOW TO TURN IT ON

M
Y W
I F E
T H I N K
S I A M G O

I N G D E A F
B U T R E A L L Y

I J U S T P R E T E N D
N O T T O H E A R H E R

I
ALW
AYSDR
EAMTOF
LOOKING

LIKEELIZA

BETHTAYLOR

IGUESSSOME

DREAMSDOCOMETRUE

I
STI
LLDR
OPACID

ALMOST

EVERYDAY

OF COURSE

NOW IT'S ANTACID

I
DO
N'TMI
NDIFPE

OPLECALL
MEABITCH

BECAUSEIN
DOGYEARSI'MONLYNINE

I

LO

OKBET

TERNOW

THANIDI

DINCOLLEGE

THANKSTOMY

PLASTICSURGEON

M
Y H
U S B A
N D S A Y S
H E ' S L I K E A

F I N E W I N E G

E T T I N G B E T T E R

W I T H A G E B U T I S A Y H E ' S

A F I N E C H E E S E G E T T I N G S M E L L I E R

K

IDS

TODAY

NEEDTO

BETAUGHT

THEMEANING

OFTHEWORDRES

PECT, THELITTLETURDS

M
Y W
I F E W
A N T S M
E T O C H E
_____
C K F O R L U M P S
"D O W N T H E R E" B U T
_____
I H A V E N' T H A D A S I G
N I F I C A N T E R E C T I O N I N Y E A R S

I

F B

Y N O W

Y O U ' V E F

O R G O T T E N

W H Y Y O U ' R E R

E A D I N G T H I S I T ' S

T I M E T O S T A R T O V E R A T

T H E B E G I N N I N G , Y O U O L D F O G E Y